Contents

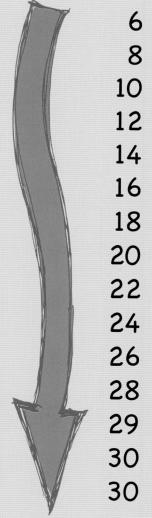

Who uses **tools?**

We all use tools. Tools help us to do our work. We choose different tools to do different jobs.

A hairdresser uses scissors to cut hair.

This car mechanic is using a drill.

A carpenter's bag is full of tools.

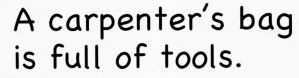

Ways into Technology

Using Tools

Written by Claire Llewellyn

W
FRANKLIN WATTS
LONDON•SYDNEY

First published in 2008 by Franklin Watts
338 Euston Road
London NW1 3BH

Franklin Watts Australia
Level 17/207 Kent Street
Sydney NSW 2000

Copyright © Franklin Watts 2008

Editor: Julia Bird
Design: Shobha Mucha
Photography: Paul Bricknell (unless
otherwise credited)
Consultant: Pam Bolton, design and technology advisor

A CIP catalogue record for this book
is available from the British Library
ISBN 978 0 7496 8081 7

Dewey Classification 621.9

Printed in China

Picture credits:
p.6: (top) Shutterstock © Nicholas Sutcliffe; (middle)
Shutterstock © Sudheer Sakthan; (bottom) istockphoto
© redmal; p.7: (top) Shutterstock © Adrian Britton;
(clockwise from top) Shutterstock © ajt; istockphoto ©
Chris Elwell; Shutterstock © Pelham James Mitchinson;
Shutterstock © Andreas Grandin; Shutterstock © Craig
Wactor; p.25: Shutterstock: © Razumovskaya Marina
Nikolaevna

Thanks to our models
Lucas Dyson-Diaz, Sophie Gunn, Kalem Patel,
Sacha Seresin and Kheilah Viljoen

Franklin Watts is a division of Hachette Children's Books,
an Hachette Livre UK company.

We use tools at home, too.

Which tools do you have at home?

Trowel

Screwdriver

Tin-opener

Hammer

Scissors

7

Using  scissors

Scissors are a very useful tool.
We use them to cut all sorts of things.

Scissors

Scissors have sharp
metal blades. When
you pull on the handles,
the blades open.
When you push them,
the blades shut.

Handles

Blades

Safety note
Always take care with scissors.
Close scissors when you are
not using them.

Lucas is making a paper decoration. He is using scissors to cut the paper.

Which of these things could you cut with scissors?

Would they be easy or hard to cut? Think before you turn the page.

Snip, snip

The woolly scarf and paper would be easy to cut with scissors.

The leather belt and the twigs would be harder to cut.

The metal spoon cannot be cut with scissors.

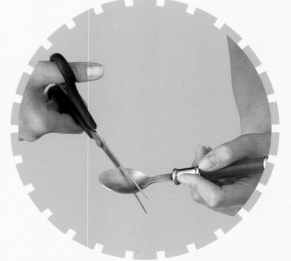

Kalem is using a tool called safety snips to cut some cardboard. Safety snips are very strong.

Safety snips

Safety snips have a safety clip. When you open the clip, the snips open. You push on the snips to cut.

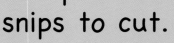

Safety clip

Blade

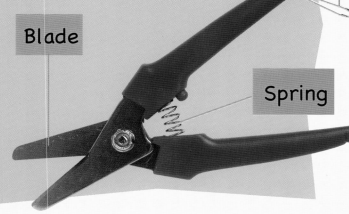

Spring

Now Kalem wants to cut a piece of wood. Wood is too hard for scissors or snips. What tool could he use instead? Think before you turn the page.

Using a  saw

Kalem can use a saw to cut wood and other hard materials.

Plastic handle

Junior hacksaw
A hacksaw has a metal blade with sharp, cutting teeth.

Metal blade

Teeth

Safety note
An adult should always be present when you are using a saw.
Always take care with a saw.
Do not walk around with a saw.
Do not talk to others when you are sawing.

Kalem measures his piece of wood and makes a mark where he needs to cut.

He puts the wood into a tool called a vice.

Kalem then pushes the saw so the teeth cut through the wood.

Vice
A vice holds wood tightly. This makes it safer to cut.

Wood is held in here

Vice is screwed to the table

Making **holes**

Tools called punches and drills help us to make holes in materials.

Sophie is making a cardboard wheel. She uses a hole punch to make a hole in it.

Punch

Hole punch
When you pull on the handles, the punch opens. When you push them, it shuts and makes a hole.

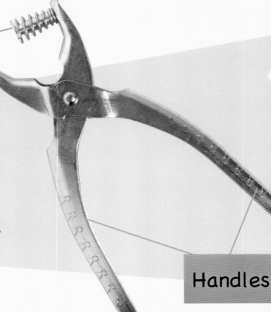

Handles

Lucas wants to add a trailer to his truck with a lolly stick. He uses a drill to make a hole in the stick.

Why is the drill on a wooden stand?

Hand drill

A hand drill has a metal bit. When you turn the handle, the bit turns and makes a hole.

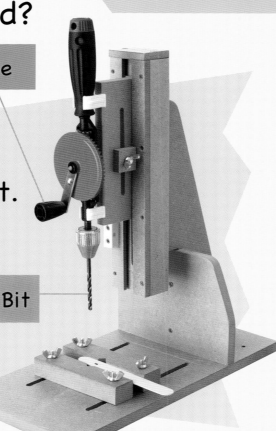

Handle

Bit

Safety note Always take care when using drills and hole punches.

Joining things

Kheilah is making a hand puppet. She needs to join two pieces of paper together. She does this with a stapler.

Stapler
A stapler punches metal clips through two surfaces.

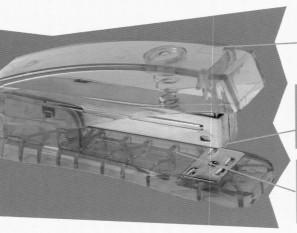

Press hard here

Staple comes out here

Put paper here

Safety note
Take care with staplers. Always use them on a table.

Another way
of joining two
surfaces is to use
a hole punch and
a split pin. That is
how Kheilah has
joined a trunk to
her elephant.

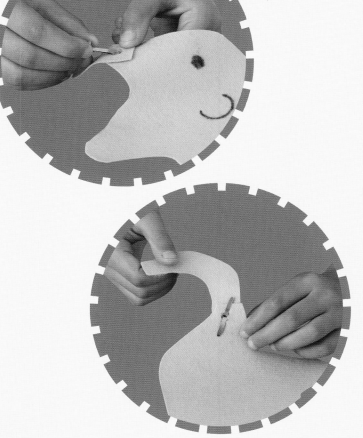

Now Kheilah is
making a purse.
She wants to join
two pieces of
cloth together.

What tools will she use? Think before
you turn the page.

Sewing tools

Kheilah uses pins and a needle and thread. These tools are used for sewing.

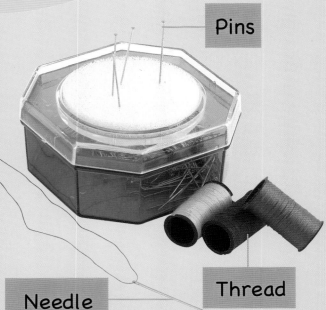

Pins

Needle

Thread

First, Kheilah pins the two pieces of cloth together. The pins hold them in place.

Then she uses a needle and thread to sew the edges together.

Sewing tools

The thread goes in the eye of the needle.

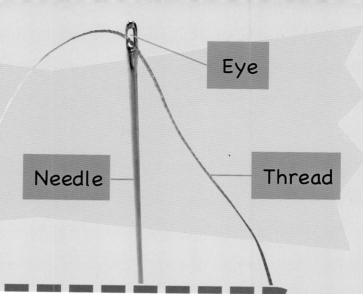

Eye

Needle

Thread

Safety note

Take care with pins and needles because they are very sharp.
Store pins in a pin cushion.
Store needles in a piece of felt.

Sacha is making a puppet. He has drawn its shape. How can he make the same shape in felt? Think what tools he needs to use before you turn the page.

A **template** is a tool

First, Sacha uses scissors to cut around his drawing. He will use the drawing as a template. A template is a useful tool.

He uses pins to join the template to two pieces of cloth.

Then he cuts around the template. He takes out the pins and removes the template.

Next, he pins the two pieces of cloth together. Finally, Sacha sews it all together, using a needle and thread.

Template

We use templates to cut shapes out of materials. What shapes could you make with these templates?

 Kitchen tools

We use many different tools in the kitchen.

Kheilah is using a peeler to peel a carrot.

Lucas is mashing a banana with a fork.

Sacha is using a spoon to put yoghurt into a dish.

22

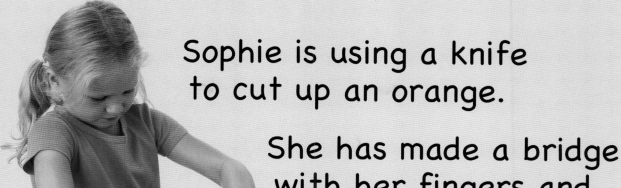

Sophie is using a knife to cut up an orange.

She has made a bridge with her fingers and is cutting the orange underneath.

Here are two more kitchen tools.

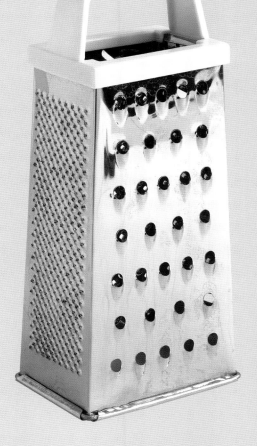

Do you know what they do?

This is a grater.
We use it to grate
cheese, carrots and other
fruit and vegetables.

This is a fruit squeezer.

We use it to squeeze
the juice out of
oranges and lemons.

Kitchen tools must be kept clean. Dirty tools can spread germs on to food, and germs can make us ill. We must wash tools after we have used them.

Then we must dry them with a clean cloth and put them away.

Where do we put tools and plates in the kitchen?

All about **tools**

Look at all the pictures on these pages.

What is the person doing in each one?

What tools are they using?

What are they doing with the tools?

How do the tools help them?

What materials are they working with?

Useful words

blade – the cutting part of a knife or other tool.

cardboard – thick, strong card that is made of paper.

carpenter – a person who makes things out of wood.

cloth – a fabric made from wool, cotton or other sort of thread.

edge – the outside part of something.

felt – a kind of cloth.

germ – a tiny living thing that can spread disease and make us feel ill.

hacksaw – a cutting tool that has a blade with teeth.

handle – the part of a tool that you hold it with.

mechanic – a person who repairs cars.

split pin – a pin with a stem that is split into two parts.

stapler – a tool for punching staples into paper.

surface – the top part of something.

template – a piece of paper cut into a special shape and used as a guide for cutting cloth or other materials.

Some answers

Here are some answers to the questions we have asked in this book. Don't worry if you had some different answers to ours; you may be right, too. Talk through your answers with other people and see if you can explain why they are right.

Page 7   There are lots of different answers to this question. Here are just three examples: garden spade, measuring tape, pliers. Ask other people what tools they have thought of.
How many tools can you think of altogether?

Page 15   The drill is on a wooden stand to keep it still. This makes it safer and easier to use.

Page 21   These templates would make the shape of a circle, a triangle and a teddy bear.

Page 25   Kitchen tools are stored in different places. Some are put away in drawers and cupboards. Others are stored in pots on the worktop or hung from hooks on the walls.

Page 26-27 Look back through the book if you need help!

Index

About this book

Ways into Technology is designed to encourage children to begin to think about how things are designed and made in the world around us. Here are some pointers to gain maximum use from **Using Tools**.

Working through this book will introduce the basic concepts about tools and how to use them and also some of the vocabulary associated with them (for example, blade, handle, edge, surface). This will prepare the child for more formal work in Design and Technology later in the school curriculum.

As you read through the book with children, ask them to point to each tool and say what it does. Discuss with children why it is important to use tools safely. What could happen otherwise?

On pages 9, 11, 17, 19 and 23, readers are invited to suggest how something might be done or predict the results of an action. Ensure that you discuss any answer they give in some depth before turning over the page. Perhaps you could set up other scenarios for the children to predict and discuss possible outcomes. For example, on page 9 you could experiment with cutting different materials. On page 23, you could try out different kitchen tools.

Pages 26-27 are an opportunity to revisit material in the book. Make sure that children are familiar with all the different names for the tools, materials and actions used throughout the book.

How Does It Work?

ENTERTAINMENT TECHNOLOGY

Linda Bruce,
Sam Bruce and
Jack Bruce

MACMILLAN
LIBRARY

First published in 2005 by
MACMILLAN EDUCATION AUSTRALIA PTY LTD
627 Chapel Street, South Yarra 3141

Visit our website at www.macmillan.com.au

Associated companies and representatives throughout the world.

National Library of Australia
Cataloguing-in-Publication data

Bruce, Linda.
Entertainment technology.

Includes index.
For upper primary school students.
ISBN 0 7329 9745 3.

1. Amusements – Juvenile literature. 2. Home entertainment
systems – Juvenile literature. I. Title. (Series: How
does it work? (South Yarra, Vic.).

793

Edited by Anna Fern
Text and cover design by Modern Art Production Group
Illustrations by Andrew Louey
Photo research by Legend Images

Printed in China

Acknowledgements
The author and publishers are grateful to the following for permission to reproduce copyright material:

Cover photo: Virtual reality game, courtesy of James King-Holmes/W Industries.

AAP, p. 23; Corbis, pp. 28, 29; AP Photo/Richard Drew, p. 16; Rob Cruse Photography, pp. 9, 15, 17; Istockphoto.com,
p. 12; Photolibrary.com, pp. 4, 5, 8, 10, 18, 20, 26; Productbank, p. 15; Reuters, pp. 6, 11; © Scott L. Robertson/
slrobertson.com , pp. 24, 25; Science Photo Library, /Antonia Reeve, p. 7, /Jerry Mason, p. 14, /James King-Holmes/
W Industries, pp. 1, 19, /Kaj R. Svensson, p. 27, /Geoff Tompkinson, p. 30; Siemens, p. 22.

While every care has been taken to trace and acknowledge copyright, the publisher tenders their apologies for any
accidental infringement where copyright has proved untraceable. Where the attempt has been unsuccessful, the publisher
welcomes information that would redress the situation.

Contents

Glossary words

When a word is printed in **bold**, you can look up its meaning in the Glossary on page 31.

What is technology?

Technology helps us to do things. Technology is also about how things work. Since ancient times, people have been interested in how things work and how they can improve technology to meet their needs. They use their experience, knowledge and ideas to invent new ways of doing things.

The *How Does It Work?* series features the design and technology of machines that are part of our daily lives. This includes:

- the purpose of the technology and its design
- where it is used
- how it is used
- materials it is made from
- how it works
- future developments.

Technology has changed the way we live in many ways. It will keep on bringing change, as people constantly invent new ways of doing things using new materials.

Entertainment technology such as pinball machines is enjoyed by people everywhere.

Entertainment technology

Entertainment technology helps us to have fun and enjoy our leisure time.

Over the past 100 years, new technology has revolutionised entertainment. Recordings on records, tapes and CDs have made music accessible across the world. Photography, film and video have enabled movies to be made and brought into our living rooms.

Ways of being entertained have changed greatly with the invention of computer technology. Many households have a personal computer, a **console** or a hand-held computer game. Computer games of endless diversity and complexity are being played on machines that are becoming tiny. Players can pit their wits against the computer or they can play against people in other parts of the world using the Internet. Fun parks utilise **simulations** and virtual reality to portray a more realistic experience.

This book takes an inside look at different kinds of entertainment technology. It also previews some amazing new inventions in entertainment technology that you might use in the future.

Virtual-reality games simulate the feeling of being inside the game.

Computer games

Computer games are interactive games that can be played on a home computer. Game types include action games, adventure games, role-playing, simulations, strategy and war games, and educational games.

Where used?

Computer games are played on home computers. They are also played on hand-held units, consoles, calculators, mobile phones and in game arcades.

How used?

Computer games can be played by a single person (with the computer as the opponent) or by groups of users who can compete against others anywhere in the world via the Internet. More powerful computers can run games with more complex **graphics** and plots.

Materials

Materials used to make computer games include metal **alloys** and plastic, which are light, durable and inexpensive. Games incorporate computer intelligence through software, **silicon chips** or other materials for recording and storing game play.

? Action and adventure games

Arcade games include shooting, fighting, racing and sport, with typical actions of running, jumping obstacles, stunning monsters or feeding them bananas and grabbing bonus points or jewels.

Platform games feature scenes, platforms and increasingly complex mazes for players to advance through, earning points as they go.

In racing games, players choose circuits, from cliff-hanging highways to shooting rapids. Speed, race time and position on the circuit are displayed on the screen.

Personal computers can run games with complex graphics and plots.

How do computer games work?

A program runs each computer game. When the player commands the game to start, the computer processes the command. It does this with its central processing unit (**CPU**), a series of **circuits** that fits on a fingernail-sized silicon chip.

mouse and keyboard
Commands are input into the game with a keyboard, mouse, joystick, steering wheel, brake, data glove or other controls.

CPU (central processing unit)
The CPU translates the program commands from binary code into sound and images on screen.

What's next?

In the future, more complex **network** games will be played against large groups of people in different parts of world. When not being played, games systems may be linked with hundreds of other computers to work on complex computing problems, such as deciphering radio signals from space.

? Bits, bytes and megabytes

Computers carry out instructions in 'binary code'. The code is measured in 'bits' which is short for 'binary digit'. Eight bits equal one byte. A megabyte is one million bytes. A game that is one gigabyte takes up 1024 megabytes of storage space. A terabyte is approximately one trillion bytes or 1024 gigabytes.

Video-game consoles

A video-game console is used to run computer games. A television is used as a display screen.

Where used?

Consoles are plugged into televisions. Over 29 million people worldwide play games on consoles. Consoles are less expensive than personal computers.

How used?

Console games can be played by a single person or by a group, each holding a game pad. To play the game, players press buttons or joysticks on the game pad. The command travels along the wire to the console. The console sends a signal to the television monitor and action appears on the television screen, together with sound.

Materials

Materials selected to make consoles include plastic casings and wire leads that do not break easily when bumped. Silicon-chip **microprocessors** run the game programs.

Unlike games on a personal computer, console games do not need to be installed and can be played immediately by inserting a game cartridge or disc.

How video-game consoles work

Video games are stored on CD, **CD-ROM** cartridges or **DVD**. The game is pushed into a slot in the console. The console contains a DVD drive, a computer (often with a built-in **hard drive**), a graphics processor, audio processor and **memory card**. The computer decodes the software and displays graphics on the television screen.

Some consoles can play DVD movies and games, and **download** games from the Internet. Others store saved games, some of which can be transferred to and played on mobile phones, calculators and personal computers.

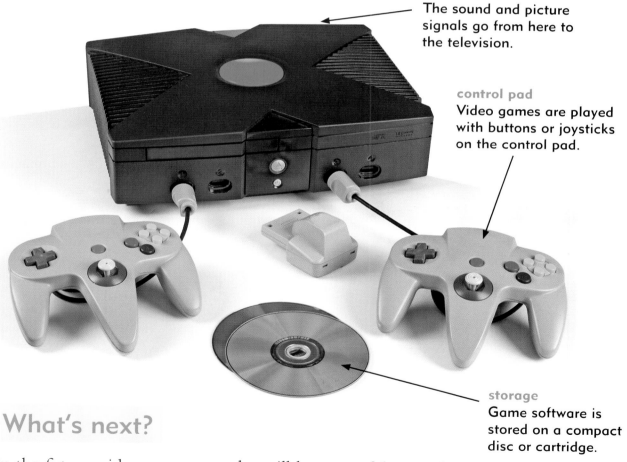

The sound and picture signals go from here to the television.

control pad
Video games are played with buttons or joysticks on the control pad.

storage
Game software is stored on a compact disc or cartridge.

What's next?

In the future, video-game consoles will be powerful enough to incorporate virtual-reality technology such as **3-D** glasses. Video-game consoles may network with other consoles across the world. Like computers, game consoles are constantly improving.

Hand-held games

Hand-held games are small, portable devices that contain built-in computer games.

Where used?

Hand-held game units are small enough to be carried in pockets. They can be used anywhere—at home, at school and while travelling.

How used?

The unit is held in one hand and the player pushes buttons to control the game action. Movements often include jumping, running, blasting obstacles, leaping onto vines and across chasms, and grabbing bonus jewels and lollypops.

Materials

The game case and screen are made of plastic, which looks good and is sturdy. They come in many fashionable colours and some people like to collect them as well as play them. Inside, the **circuitry** includes silicon chips and metal wiring.

Battery-operated hand-held games can be played anywhere.

How hand-held games work

Hand-held games have built-in games and a tiny computer powered by batteries. The games often require hand–eye coordination to move bats under balls or fit moving blocks into holes. They also feature action figures, which players command to jump, run, throw and shoot.

liquid crystal display
The screen may display 32 000 shades of colour.

controls
The game is played by pressing the directional pad and left and right shoulder buttons.

speaker

batteries
Inside the game, two AA disposable or rechargeable batteries allow up to 20 hours of playing time.

SELECT   START

What's next?

In the future, games with wireless radio connections will enable two players, each with a hand-held game, to compete against each other.

Compact-disc games

Compact–disc games feature complex images and sound stored on a CD-ROM or DVD.

Where used?

Compact–disc games are played on personal computers, often at home.

How used?

The disc is placed in the disc drive, the game launches and the player follows on–screen game instructions to play the game. The game can be viewed on a computer and copied from disc to computer, but the information on the disc itself cannot be changed. A DVD can hold at least seven times more information than a CD-ROM. DVDs hold games, encyclopedias or movies that would otherwise require multiple CDs with constant disc changing during playing.

Materials

Discs are made from polycarbonate plastic with a thin layer of **aluminium**.

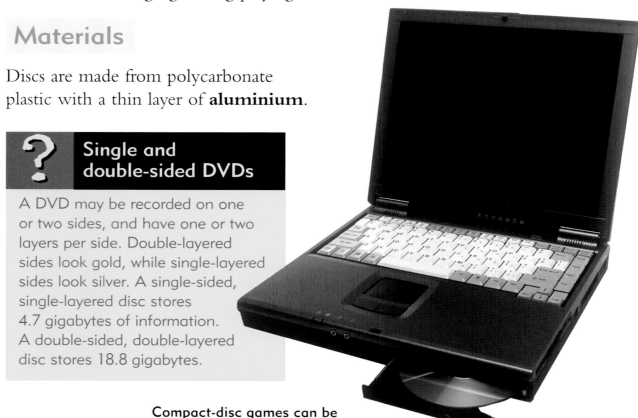

? Single and double-sided DVDs

A DVD may be recorded on one or two sides, and have one or two layers per side. Double-layered sides look gold, while single-layered sides look silver. A single-sided, single-layered disc stores 4.7 gigabytes of information. A double-sided, double-layered disc stores 18.8 gigabytes.

Compact-disc games can be played on laptops and personal computers.

How do compact disc games work?

The information on a compact disc is stored as a track of tiny bumps which spiral out from the centre of the disc. When the disc is placed in the disc drive, it spins at between 200 and 500 revolutions per minute. A **laser** light inside the player follows the spiral track. The reflective surface of the CD reflects the laser light off the bumps so that the player can read the disc and convert the digital information into sound and video.

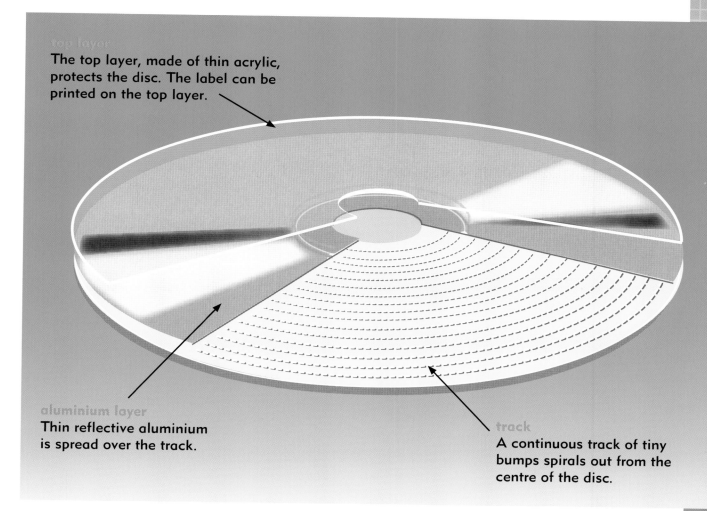

top layer
The top layer, made of thin acrylic, protects the disc. The label can be printed on the top layer.

aluminium layer
Thin reflective aluminium is spread over the track.

track
A continuous track of tiny bumps spirals out from the centre of the disc.

What's next?

In the future, smaller discs and memory cards will store much more information.

CD and DVD players

A CD or DVD player uses a laser to read a compact disc and translate this information into graphics and sound. CD and DVD players can play music, videos, computer games, computer programs and most other digitally encoded information.

Where used?

Some CD and DVD players can be used as a separate unit, or they can be connected to a television or sound system. They are often built into personal computers and game consoles.

How used?

When the disc is placed in the player, the drive reads the disc. The CD or DVD player can be controlled by pushing controls on the player, or by giving commands through a remote control, keyboard, mouse, joystick or other input device.

Materials

Materials selected include sturdy metal wiring, a protective plastic case and a laser light to read tiny tracks on the disc.

CD and DVD players can read and play back digital entertainment.

How CD and DVD players work

CD and DVD players read information stored as bumps on the disc and translate them into images and sound. Attached to the CD or DVD player, a screen displays graphics and speakers play the sound.

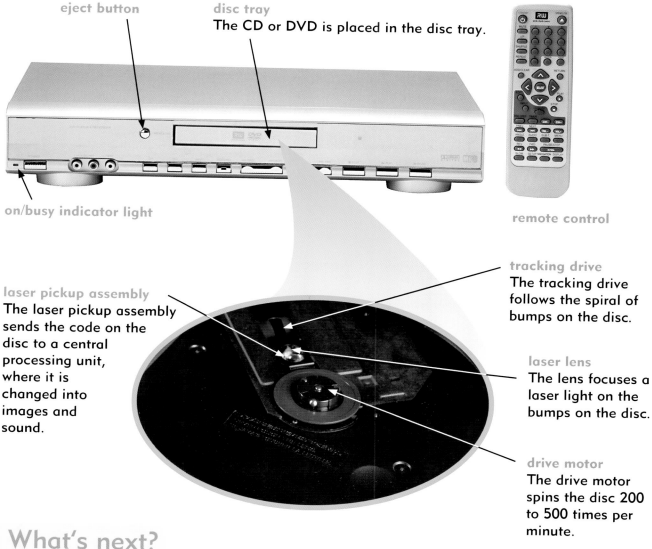

eject button

disc tray
The CD or DVD is placed in the disc tray.

on/busy indicator light

remote control

laser pickup assembly
The laser pickup assembly sends the code on the disc to a central processing unit, where it is changed into images and sound.

tracking drive
The tracking drive follows the spiral of bumps on the disc.

laser lens
The lens focuses a laser light on the bumps on the disc.

drive motor
The drive motor spins the disc 200 to 500 times per minute.

What's next?

In the future, faster Internet connections may enable games, music or movies to be accessed over the Internet instead of being stored on discs and played by individual disc drives. Players will pay to access the game, run the movie or download the music. Discs will not be needed.

Pocket MPEG players

A pocket MPEG player can be used to watch movies, listen to music or play games.

Where used?

MPEG players can be used anywhere. They are small enough to be carried in a pocket, or to be clipped to a belt or armband.

How used?

The user presses buttons on the case to input commands, such as selecting a program, video or game. MPEG entertainment can be bought on CD or DVD or downloaded from the Internet. The MPEG player can be connected by a lead to a personal computer so that entertainment can be transferred from the computer to the player.

Materials

The MPEG player case is made of strong plastic. Inside, the circuitry includes a silicon chip for reading and playing the program and wires made from metal alloys. MPEG players are made with a minimum of moving parts so that play is unaffected by movement.

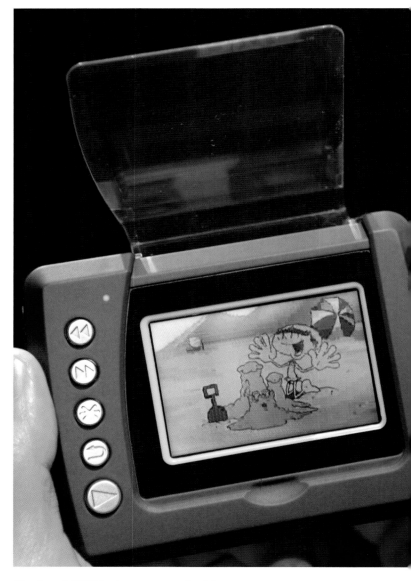

Pocket MPEG players can hold games, movies, TV and songs.

How do MPEG players work?

MPEG players have a mini-computer for storing and playing digital MPEG entertainment. Inside the player, a microprocessor reads MPEG encoded entertainment, and plays it over a display. The display can be a small built-in screen or sometimes the MPEG player can be connected to an external screen.

personal computer

Music can be downloaded from the Internet via a personal computer. When the data has been downloaded, a cable is plugged from the computer to the MPEG player and the music can be copied across to the MPEG player.

CPU

Inside, the CPU (central processing unit) reads the digital information stored on the MPEG player and changes it into sound and pictures.

cable

The cable enables MPEG files to be transferred from the computer to the MPEG player.

What's next?

In the future, MPEG players will have sharper pictures and will be cheaper. More players will link with other people's MPEG players using a wireless connection.

Virtual-reality games

A virtual-reality game uses a computer to create the experience of being inside the game itself.

Where used?

Virtual-reality (VR) games are played at home with a personal computer and in video arcades and theme parks.

How used?

Players wear VR equipment designed to create experiences such as sound, touch and movement. Equipment may include display screens, 3-D masks, data gloves and devices such as waist tethers to tell the computer where the player is within the game. Movement detectors built into head displays enable the computer to create views that players would see as they turn their head and walk within the game. For example, players can view birds swooping or a monster following them.

Materials

Materials selected to make VR equipment include metal, plastic and silicon chips.

Virtual-reality headsets provide views for each direction in which a player looks.

How do virtual-reality games work?

Virtual reality enables players to move around in a computer-generated 3-D environment. Realistic, 3-D holographic images are created by a video being projected onto a special surface. Players may compete against life-size **holograms** of people, animals and monsters, or see virtual racing cars whiz past.

headset
The headset provides a view of the direction in which the player looks.

data glove
The data glove enables the player to move their hand inside the game.

waist sensor
The waist sensor detects the player's position.

playing platform
The playing platform defines where the action takes place.

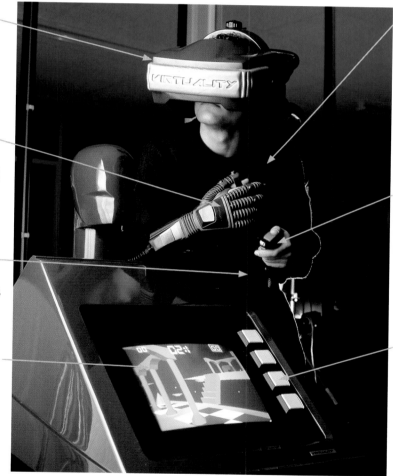

vest
The vest can detect and record when you have been hit by an **infra-red light** beam from another player's laser gun.

equipment
Players may use laser guns, steering wheels or other virtual-reality equipment.

computer software system

What's next?

In the future, VR technology for home use will include headsets with stereo sound and vision, games that respond to voice commands and holograms to create scenes around players. VR goggles will display 3-D images which change in response to the user's actions and positions.

3-D glasses

Watching 3-D movies requires the viewer to wear 3-D glasses. The glasses provide viewers with a realistic experience of visual depth.

Where used?

People use 3-D glasses to watch 3-D movies at home and in public cinemas. 3-D movies are made up of two images projected onto a screen. 3-D glasses allow only one image to enter each eye, and you see this as depth.

How used?

Watching a 3-D movie can make the action seem so realistic that, for example, viewers feel that they are walking on the edge of a cliff, or that animals come so close that they can be touched. Without 3-D glasses, a 3-D movie looks blurred.

Materials

One type of 3-D glasses is made with sturdy plastic frames and lenses. Other 3-D glasses are made from paper and coloured cellophane, which is inexpensive, flexible and light to wear.

3-D movies can seem so realistic that audiences feel they are part of the action on the screen.

How do 3-D glasses work?

We see depth around us because each of our two eyes sees slightly different images. 3-D glasses create the impression of depth by feeding a different image into each eye.

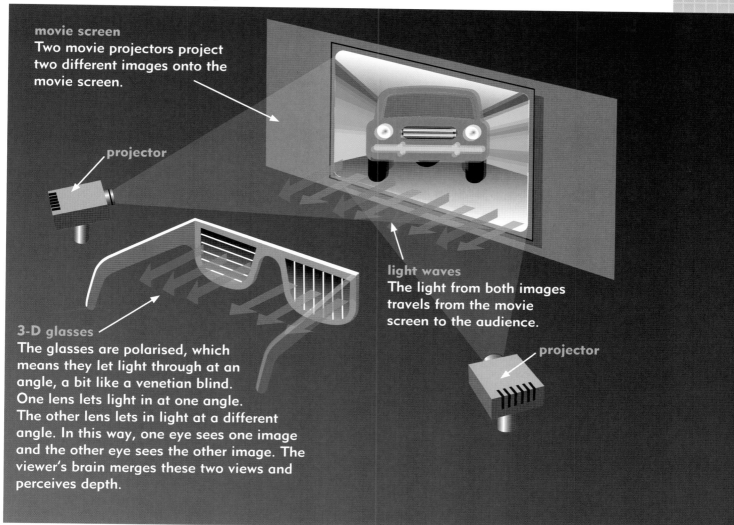

movie screen
Two movie projectors project two different images onto the movie screen.

projector

3-D glasses
The glasses are polarised, which means they let light through at an angle, a bit like a venetian blind. One lens lets light in at one angle. The other lens lets in light at a different angle. In this way, one eye sees one image and the other eye sees the other image. The viewer's brain merges these two views and perceives depth.

light waves
The light from both images travels from the movie screen to the audience.

projector

What's next?

In the future, movies may use holograms and virtual-reality technology to enable viewers to feel like they are walking around inside the action. Instead of being projected onto a screen in a large theatre, movies will be screened into the viewers' goggles.

Augmented reality

Augmented-reality systems add or join graphics, sounds, and even the sense of touch and smell to the natural world. In augmented reality, computer graphics are overlaid onto a live video picture, or projected onto a transparent screen such as in a head-up display. In this way extra information is added to what is being experienced.

Where used?

Augmented reality is in its early stages of development. It has been used in computer games, in some hi-tech museums as a tourist attraction, and in the military to help troops find their way around and to identify buildings and objects.

How used?

Augmented-reality glasses overlay information and sound on a normal view. They may be linked to **satellite** global positioning systems.

Materials

Augmented-reality devices may involve special glasses or headsets that are sensitive to place, using small computing and display devices. Materials are selected to be easy to maintain, safe and comfortable to use.

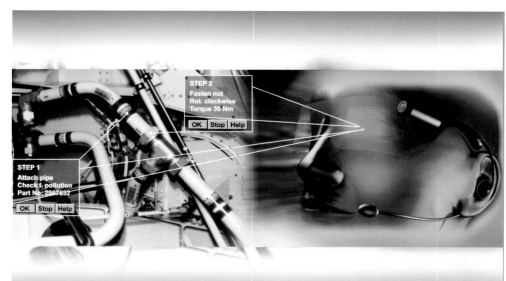

Augmented-reality adds graphics and sounds to the real world.

How augmented reality works

Augmented-reality graphics are coordinated so they change with the wearer's head movements. Augmented-reality systems recognise objects the wearer is looking at, and display information about that view in the wearer's goggles. For example, in an augmented-reality game, you may find yourself racing a virtual car against a real televised race on television.

tracking system
A personal locator uses a satellite signal to locate a person in their surroundings in order to provide correct information.

head-mounted display
A see-through overlay displays text and graphics as well as the wearer's natural surroundings. Sound is also added. Other devices may be used to simulate touch or even smell.

Small batteries in the player's backpack provide power. A built-in mobile computer processes the data.

What's next?

In the future, augmented reality technology may focus on a person's inner state as well as their surroundings. For example, if a person is stressed, calming images and instructions may be superimposed to help them cope better.

Slingshot rides

The slingshot ride simulates a rocket launch by propelling a capsule attached to steel cables straight up into the air.

Where used?

This ride is used in amusement parks. Every ride has safety rules, and there are often restrictions on riders' age, height and weight, and warnings for people who suffer from medical conditions such as weak hearts or neck injuries.

How used?

Riders sit in a metal capsule. Metal bars hold them into their seats. The capsule tilts so riders are lying on their backs. A loudspeaker counts down '3, 2, 1'. Then the **magnet** releases and the capsule shoots over 100 metres high and more than 40 metres past the top of the support towers.

Materials

The springs, ropes and pulleys of the ride are made from strong steel.

The sling-shot ride shoots capsule riders into the air.

How slingshot rides work

The slingshot capsule sits on a specially designed, powerful spring held down by a huge magnet. When the magnet is turned off, the capsule launches straight up at speeds of over 160 kilometres per hour. A computer senses spring tension and ensures that every rider, whether light or heavy, receives an equal amount of thrust. When the capsule returns, the spring machine hurls it back up again, flipping the capsule over and over.

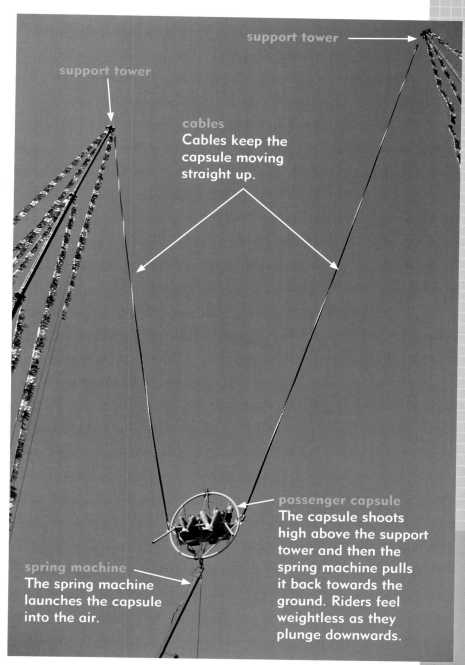

support tower

support tower

cables
Cables keep the capsule moving straight up.

passenger capsule
The capsule shoots high above the support tower and then the spring machine pulls it back towards the ground. Riders feel weightless as they plunge downwards.

spring machine
The spring machine launches the capsule into the air.

What's next?

In the future, amusement parks may have rocket sleds that hit **hypersonic** speeds of Mach 8.5, or 10 352 kilometres per hour.

Roller-coasters

A roller-coaster ride provides excitement, unexpected twists, turns and dips, and a sense of danger while being completely safe for riders.

Where used?

Roller-coasters are found in amusement parks. Invented in the United States of America, they are popular all over the world.

How used?

Riders sit in cars, with a bar over their lap to hold them so they cannot fall out.

The coaster is towed to the top of a steep track. Then it descends, racing around sharp bends creating a feeling of danger for the riders. Finally, it stops back at the station.

Materials

Roller-coasters are mainly made from metals that are strong, durable, easy to maintain and minimally affected by changes of condition. Tracks are made from long steel tubes supported by strong, light, slightly larger steel tubes or beams. The coaster wheels are made from strong man-made substances such as polyurethane or nylon.

Roller-coasters give riders the exciting feeling that they are in danger.

How roller-coasters work

Roller-coasters are dragged to the top of a track by a motor. Once at the top of the track, the roller-coaster uses **gravity** to speed down the track, going faster and faster. As the ride progresses, the track continually loses height, which causes the roller-coaster to speed up, and gains height, which makes it slow down.

Preventing collisions

Electromagnet sensors in the roller-coaster track prevent train collision by detecting metal 'flags' on the trains. Flags on the front and rear of the train tell the computer the train has entered and left a particular section of the track.

clamps
When the roller-coaster is upside down, it is rigidly attached to the track.

brakes
Brakes built into the track clamp closed on metal fins running under the train to slow the roller-coaster.

wheels
Wheels on top of the track keep the train running smoothly. Wheels under the track and along the sides anchor the car to the track during dips and turns.

track

What's next?

In the future, higher, faster roller-coasters may be combined with even scarier video backdrops, such as going inside a volcano or over cliffs.

Pendulum rides

A pendulum ride is like a swing. It gradually swings higher and higher and sometimes completes a circle.

Where used?

Pendulum rides are found in amusement parks all over the world.

How used?

Riders step from the station platform into a capsule. Bars around their arms and body prevent them from falling out. The capsule swings in an increasing arc until it completes a full circle. It then rocks back to a stop at the completion of the ride. When the ride completes a 360-degree circle, the capsule turns upside down and riders experience a feeling of complete weightlessness.

Materials

The capsule swing may be made from moulded metal and heavy-duty synthetic materials. Cables are made from strong steel. These materials require little maintenance and can withstand heat, cold, rain and wind.

Pendulum rides swing higher and higher until they complete a full circle.

How pendulum rides work

Pendulum rides swing a capsule in an arc between two main towers. At the bottom of the arc, pendulum riders experience a feeling of high gravity forces as they are pressed into their seats. At the top of the arc, riders feel weightless, as the seat is not pressing on them and they are free-falling.

capsule
The capsule swings along the track in an increasing arc, pausing at the top of each arc before it is pulled back down by gravity. When high enough, the capsule sometimes completes a full circle.

safety bar
Riders are held in their seats by a metal bar.

entry platform
Riders step into the capsule here.

What's next?

In the future, pendulum rides may swing between 50-storey-high towers. Virtual reality may give riders the exact experience of being on a pendulum ride without leaving the ground.

How well does it work?

In this book you have read about and looked at the designs of many different technologies. As well as understanding how technology works, we also need to think about how well it works in relation to other needs, such as aesthetic, environmental and social needs. We can judge how well the idea, product or process works by considering questions such as:

Manufacture	• Is the manufacture of the technology efficient in its use of energy and resources?
Usability	• Does the technology do the job it is designed to do? • Is it safe to use? • Is it easy to use?
Social impact	• Does it have any negative effects on people?
Environmental impact	• Does using the technology have any environmental effects? • Does it create noise, cause pollution or create any waste products?
Aesthetics	• Does the design fit into its surroundings and look attractive?

Thinking about these sorts of questions can help people to invent improved ways of doing things.

Virtual reality and simulated experiences bring a new level of thrills to computer-game technology.

Glossary

alloys mixtures of metals

aluminium a strong, light metal which resists rust and conducts electricity and heat well

CD-ROM (compact disc read only memory) a disc that can store up to 650 megabytes of data

circuits paths between two or more points along which an electrical current or signal can be carried

circuitry a system of electrical circuits

console a device used for direct communication with a computer system

CPU (Central Processing Unit) the silicon chip 'brain' of the computer— the more powerful the chip, the faster programs run

download copy file from a central Internet server

DVD (digital versatile disc) physically similar to a CD, a DVD can store up to 17 gigabytes of data

electromagnet a magnet that needs electricity to activate it

graphics anything displayed on a computer screen that is not text

gravity a force that pulls objects back to the surface of the Earth

hard drive the main device in a computer that is used to permanently store and retrieve information

holograms flat images that appear to be three-dimensional

hypersonic speeds of five times the speed of sound (Mach 5) or higher

infra-red light a wavelength of electromagnetic radiation that is similar to the wavelength of red light, but which is invisible to the human eye

laser a highly focused beam of light which can produce immense heat and power when focused at close range

magnet metal that can pull iron or steel objects towards it and hold or move them

memory card a credit-card-sized card that can store digital data

microprocessor the central processing unit (CPU) or silicon-chip 'brain' of a computer

network a group of connected computers that can communicate with one another

satellite a machine placed in orbit around Earth to perform a job, such as relaying communications signals

silicon chip a wafer-thin slice of silicon, smaller than a finger nail, which contains thousands of microscopic electronic circuits

simulations computer games that imitate a real-world experience.

3-D (three dimensional) having, or appearing to have, length, width and depth

uploaded to copy a file from a personal computer to an Internet server

Index